Easy Home Cooking™

SLOW COOKER
Recipes

PUBLICATIONS INTERNATIONAL, LTD.

CROCK–POT is a registered trademark of The Rival Company.

Photography: Sanders Studios, Inc.
Photographer: Kathy Sanders
Photographer's Assistant: Cristin Nestor
Prop Stylist: Patty Higgins
Food Stylists: Donna Coates, Gail O'Donnell
Assistant Food Stylist: Kim Hartman
Studio Coordinator: Kathy Ores

Pictured on the front cover: Favorite Beef Stew *(page 42).*

Pictured on the back cover *(clockwise from top left):* Caponata *(page 12),* Poached Pears with Raspberry Sauce *(page 88)* and Mediterranean Gumbo *(page 66).*

ISBN: 0-7853-2390-2

Manufactured in U.S.A.

8 7 6 5 4 3 2 1

Nutritional Analysis: Nutritional information is given for the recipes in this publication. Each analysis is based on the food items in the ingredient list, except ingredients labeled as "optional" or "for garnish." When more than one ingredient choice is listed, the first ingredient is used for analysis. If a range for the amount of an ingredient is given, the nutritional analysis is based on the lowest amount. Foods offered as "serve with" suggestions are not included in the analysis unless otherwise stated.

Slow Cooker Recipes

The Basics   6

Glossary   11

Appetizers & Beverages   12

Get the party started with these fabulous, no-fuss snacks and drinks

p. 20

p. 50

Main Courses   24

Warm & wonderful dinners ready and waiting for you

Soups & Side Dishes   60

A sampling of hearty & satisfying soups and side dishes

Breads & Desserts   82

Old-fashioned pleasures to complete any meal

Index   94

p. 86

The Basics

Slow cookers can prepare just about any type of food you can imagine. Hearty soups and stews, creative chicken, pork and beef recipes, exciting party ideas and old-fashioned breads and desserts are all included in this publication. Inviting the family over for a relaxed Sunday afternoon meal? Surprise them with Thai Turkey & Noodles. Have a case of the winter blues? A comforting beef stew can be just the right thing. Need an easy dessert? Poached Pears with Raspberry Sauce fits the bill. By following these easy and enticing recipes, you can prepare wonderful meals without a lot of fuss, bother or time.

Slow cookers were introduced in the 1970s and are finding renewed popularity in the 1990s.

Considering the hectic pace of today's lifestyle, it's no wonder so many people have rediscovered this time-saving kitchen helper. Spend a few minutes preparing the ingredients, turn on the slow cooker and relax. Long cooking times without any fuss take the stress out of meal preparation.

Leave for work or a day of leisure and return 4, 8 or even 10 hours later for a hot, delicious meal.

ABOUT SLOW COOKERS

The original and best-selling slow cooker is The Rival Company's Crock-Pot® Slow Cooker. The name "Crock-Pot®" is often used interchangeably with "slow cooker."

There are two types of slow cookers. The most popular models, including the Crock-Pot® Slow Cooker, have heat coils circling

Slow cookers come in a variety of sizes and styles.

the crockery insert, allowing heat to surround the food and cook evenly. The LOW (about 200°F) and HIGH (about 300°F) settings regulate cooking temperature. One hour on HIGH equals 2 to 2½ hours on LOW. Every recipe in this publication was developed for slow cooking in the 3½-quart Rival® Crock-Pot® Slow Cooker. Less common models of slow cookers have heat coils only on the bottom and have an adjustable thermostat. If you own this type, consult your manufacturer's instructions for advice on converting recipes.

THE BENEFITS

● No need for constant attention or frequent stirring

● No worry about burning or overcooking

● No sink full of pots and pans to scrub at the end of a long day

● Great for parties and buffets

● Keeps your kitchen cool by keeping your oven turned off

● Saves energy—cooking on the low setting uses less energy than most light bulbs

THE BASICS

● As with conventional cooking recipes, slow cooker recipe time ranges are provided to account for variables such as temperature of ingredients before cooking, how full the slow cooker is and even

altitude. Once you become familiar with your slow cooker you'll have a good idea which end of the time range to use.

● Manufacturers recommend that slow cookers should be one-half to three-quarters full for best results.

● Keep a lid on it! The slow cooker can take as long as twenty minutes to regain the heat lost when the cover is removed. If the recipe calls for stirring or checking the dish near the end of the cooking time, replace the lid as quickly as you can.

● To clean your slow cooker, follow the manufacturer's instructions. To make cleanup even easier, spray with nonstick cooking spray before adding food.

● Always taste the finished dish before serving and adjust seasonings to your preference. Consider adding a dash of any of the following: salt, pepper, seasoned salt, seasoned herb blends, lemon juice, soy sauce, Worcestershire sauce, flavored vinegar, freshly ground pepper or minced fresh herbs.

TIPS AND TECHNIQUES

Adapting Recipes: If you'd like to adapt your own favorite recipe to a slow cooker, you'll need to follow a few guidelines. First, try to find a similar recipe in this publication or your manufacturer's guide. Note the cooking times, liquid, quantity and size of meat and vegetable pieces. Because the slow cooker captures moisture, you will want to reduce the amount of liquid, often by as much as half. Add dairy products toward the end of the cooking time so they do not curdle. Follow the chart below to estimate the cooking time you will need.

Selecting the Right Meat: A good tip to keep in mind while shopping is that you can, and in fact should, use tougher, inexpensive cuts of meat. Top-quality cuts, such as loin chops or filet mignon, fall apart during long cooking periods. Keep those for roasting, broiling or grilling and save money when you use your slow cooker. You will be amazed to find even the toughest cuts come out fork-tender and flavorful.

Reducing Fat: The slow cooker can help you make meals lower in fat because you won't be cooking in fat as you do when you stir-fry and sauté. And tougher cuts of meat have less fat than prime cuts. Many recipes contain less than 30% calories from fat.

Use a sharp knife to cut away any visible fat.

TIME GUIDE

If Recipe Says:	Cook on Low:*	or	Cook on High:
15 to 30 minutes	4 to 6 hours		1½ to 2 hours
35 to 45 minutes	6 to 10 hours		3 to 4 hours
50 minutes to 3 hours	8 to 18 hours		4 to 6 hours

*Most uncooked meat and vegetable combinations will require at least 8 hours on LOW.
*Reprinted with permission from **Rival's Crock-Pot**® **Slow Cooke**r instruction book.*

If you do use fatty cuts, such as ribs, consider browning them first on top of the range to cook off excess fat.

Chicken skin tends to shrivel and curl in the slow cooker; therefore, most recipes call for skinless chicken. If you use skin-on pieces, brown them before adding them to the slow cooker. If you would rather remove the skin, use the technique shown below.

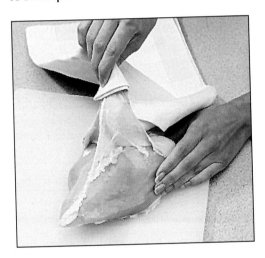

Freeze chicken until firm, but not hard. (Do not refreeze thawed chicken.) Grasp skin with clean cotton kitchen towel or paper towel and pull away from meat, discard skin. When finished skinning chicken, launder towel before using again.

You can easily remove most of the fat from accumulated juices, soups and canned broths. The simplest way is to refrigerate the liquid for several hours or overnight. The fat will congeal and float to the top for easy removal. If you plan to use the liquid right away, ladle it into a bowl or measuring cup. Let it stand about 5 minutes so the fat can rise to the surface. Skim with a large spoon. You can also lightly pull a sheet of clean paper towel over the surface, letting the grease be absorbed. To degrease canned broth, refrigerate the unopened can. Simply spoon the congealed fat off the surface after opening the can.

Cutting Your Vegetables:
Vegetables often take longer to cook than meats. Cut vegetables into small, thin pieces and place them on the bottom or near the sides of the slow cooker. Pay careful attention to the recipe instructions in order to cut vegetables to the proper size.

Cut carrots into ½-inch-thick slices.

Foil to the Rescue: To easily lift a dish or a meat loaf out of the slow cooker, make foil handles according to the following directions.

Tear off three 18×3-inch strips of heavy-duty foil. Crisscross the strips so they resemble the spokes of a wheel. Place your dish or food in the center of the strips.

Pull the foil strips up and place into the slow cooker. Leave them in while you cook so you can easily lift the item out again when ready.

Food Safety Tips: If you do any advance preparation, such as trimming meat or cutting vegetables, make sure you keep the food covered and refrigerated until you're ready to start cooking. Store uncooked meats and vegetables separately. If you are preparing meat, poultry or fish, remember to wash your cutting board, utensils and hands before touching other foods.

Once your dish is cooked, don't keep it in the slow cooker too long. Foods need to be kept cooler than 40°F or hotter than 140°F to avoid the growth of harmful bacteria. Remove food to a clean container and cover and refrigerate as soon as possible. *Do not reheat leftovers in the slow cooker.* Use a microwave oven, the range-top or the oven for reheating.

By following these simple techniques and using the exciting recipes in this publication, you will soon be preparing wonderful dishes with minimal effort.

Ancho Chili Pepper: Dried pepper ranging in intensity from mild to strong. When fresh, it is called a poblano chili pepper.

Andouille: Large spicy sausage, usually smoked, made of pork and tripe. Popular in Cajun cuisine, it is traditionally used in gumbo and jambalaya.

Au Gratin: French cooking term referring to foods topped with cheese or bread crumbs and browned under a broiler.

Bratwurst: German-style sausage made with seasoned pork and/or veal.

Brisket: Cut of beef taken from the breast portion of the cow. It is often used to make corned beef.

Caper: Unripened flower bud of a shrub native to the Mediterranean. The buds are dried and then preserved in vinegar brine.

Cheesecloth: Cotton cloth used most often to make a pouch to hold seasonings or to line molds. It can be purchased in supermarkets, hardware stores and gourmet shops.

Converted Rice: Rice that has been briefly boiled or steamed by the manufacturer to remove excess starch. It takes slightly longer to cook than regular rice but makes rice that is fluffy rather than sticky.

Couscous: Quick-cooking semolina pasta that looks like small grains of rice. It is a staple of North African cuisine.

Cut in: Technique used to mix a solid fat with dry ingredients to make uniform pieces. A wire pastry blender or two knives are usually used. It can also be done in a food processor by pulsing it on and off.

Fennel: Feathery-looking herb with a slight licorice flavor. It can be purchased fresh or dried either as whole or ground seeds.

Lentil: Legume roughly the size of a small dried pea.

Parsnip: Sweet, starchy root vegetable that can be prepared in the same manner as potatoes.

Pork Butt: Comes from the shoulder of the pig. It is also called Boston butt or shoulder blade roast.

Ragoût: French term referring to a thick stew.

Tabbouleh: Middle Eastern dish of bulgur wheat flavored with tomatoes, onions, parsley, mint and lemon. Tabbouleh mix can be purchased in supermarkets.

Tomatillo: Green fruit with a papery husk that is similar to a tomato. It is popular in Latin American, Mexican and Southwestern U.S. cuisines.

Appetizers & Beverages

Caponata

1 medium eggplant (about 1 pound), peeled and cut into ½-inch pieces

1 can (14½ ounces) diced Italian plum tomatoes, undrained

1 medium onion, chopped

1 red bell pepper, cut into ½-inch pieces

½ cup prepared medium-hot salsa

¼ cup extra-virgin olive oil

2 tablespoons capers, drained

2 tablespoons balsamic vinegar

1 teaspoon dried oregano leaves

3 cloves garlic, minced

¼ teaspoon salt

⅓ cup packed fresh basil, cut into thin strips

Toasted sliced Italian or French bread

MIX all ingredients except basil and bread in slow cooker. Cover and cook on LOW 7 to 8 hours or until vegetables are crisp-tender. Stir in basil. Serve at room temperature with toasted bread.

Makes about 5¼ cups

Nutrients per Serving: *Calories 42, Total Fat 3 g, Protein <1 g, Carbohydrate 4 g, Cholesterol 0 mg, Sodium 141 mg, Dietary Fiber <1 g Dietary Exchanges: 1 Vegetable, ½ Fat*

Mulled Apple Cider

2 quarts bottled apple cider
or juice (not unfiltered)
¼ cup packed brown sugar
1 square (8 inches) double-
thickness cheesecloth
8 allspice berries

4 cinnamon sticks, broken
into halves
12 whole cloves
1 large orange
Additional cinnamon
sticks (optional)

COMBINE apple cider and brown sugar in slow cooker. Rinse cheesecloth; squeeze out water. Wrap allspice berries and cinnamon stick halves in cheesecloth; tie securely with cotton string or strip of cheesecloth. Stick cloves randomly into orange; cut orange into quarters. Place spice bag and orange quarters in juice mixture. Cover and cook on HIGH 2½ to 3 hours. Once cooked, cider may be turned to LOW and kept warm up to 3 additional hours. Discard spice bag and orange quarters; ladle cider into mugs. Garnish with additional cinnamon sticks, if desired.   *Makes 10 servings*

Nutrients per Serving: Calories 120, Total Fat <1 g, Protein <1 g, Carbohydrate 33 g, Cholesterol 0 mg, Sodium 8 mg, Dietary Fiber <1 g
Dietary Exchanges: 2 Fruit

KITCHEN HOW-TO

To make inserting cloves into the orange a little easier, first pierce the orange skin with point of wooden skewer. Remove the skewer and insert a clove.

Chili con Queso

1 pound pasteurized
   process cheese spread,
   cut into cubes
1 can (10 ounces) diced
   tomatoes and green
   chilies, undrained
1 cup sliced green onions
2 teaspoons ground
   coriander

2 teaspoons ground cumin
¾ teaspoon hot pepper
   sauce
Green onion strips
   (optional)
Hot pepper slices
   (optional)

COMBINE all ingredients except green onion strips and hot pepper slices in slow cooker until well blended. Cover and cook on LOW 2 to 3 hours or until hot.* Garnish with green onion strips and hot pepper slices, if desired.

Makes 3 cups

*Chili will be very hot; use caution when serving.

Nutrients per Serving: Calories 233, Total Fat 16 g, Protein 13 g, Carbohydrate 10 g, Cholesterol 43 mg, Sodium 1208 mg, Dietary Fiber <1 g
Dietary Exchanges: 2 Vegetable, 1½ Meat, 2 Fat

Cook's Nook

Serve Chili con Queso with tortilla chips. Or, for something different, cut pita bread into triangles and toast in preheated 400°F oven for 5 minutes or until crisp.

Mocha Supreme

2 quarts brewed strong
    coffee
½ cup instant hot chocolate
    beverage mix
1 cinnamon stick, broken
    into halves

1 cup whipping cream
1 tablespoon powdered
    sugar

PLACE coffee, hot chocolate mix and cinnamon stick halves in slow cooker; stir. Cover and cook on HIGH 2 to 2½ hours or until hot. Remove and discard cinnamon stick halves.

BEAT cream in medium bowl with electric mixer on high speed until soft peaks form. Add powdered sugar; beat until stiff peaks form. Ladle hot beverage into mugs; top with whipped cream.

Makes 8 servings

Nutrients per Serving: Calories 132, Total Fat 12 g, Protein 1 g, Carbohydrate 7 g, Cholesterol 41 mg, Sodium 51 mg, Dietary Fiber <1 g
Dietary Exchanges: ½ Bread, 2 Fat

Cook's Nook

You can whip cream faster if you first chill the beaters and bowl in the freezer for 15 minutes.

Barbecued Meatballs

....

2 pounds lean ground beef
1⅓ cups ketchup, divided
3 tablespoons seasoned
    dry bread crumbs
1 egg, slightly beaten
2 tablespoons dried onion
    flakes
¾ teaspoon garlic salt
½ teaspoon black pepper
1 cup packed brown sugar

1 can (6 ounces) tomato
    paste
¼ cup reduced-sodium soy
    sauce
¼ cup cider vinegar
1½ teaspoons hot pepper
    sauce
Diced bell peppers
    (optional)

PREHEAT oven to 350°F. Combine ground beef, ⅓ cup ketchup, bread crumbs, egg, onion flakes, garlic salt and black pepper in medium bowl. Mix lightly but thoroughly; shape into 1-inch meatballs. Place meatballs in two 15×10-inch jelly-roll pans or shallow roasting pans. Bake 18 minutes or until browned. Transfer meatballs to slow cooker.

MIX remaining 1 cup ketchup, sugar, tomato paste, soy sauce, vinegar and hot pepper sauce in medium bowl. Pour over meatballs. Cover and cook on LOW 4 hours. Serve with cocktail picks. Garnish with bell peppers, if desired.   *Makes about 4 dozen meatballs*

Variation: For Barbecued Franks, arrange 2 (12-ounce) packages or 3 (8-ounce) packages cocktail franks in slow cooker. Combine 1 cup ketchup, sugar, tomato paste, soy sauce, vinegar and hot pepper sauce in medium bowl; pour over franks. Cook according to directions for Barbecued Meatballs.

Nutrients per Serving: Calories 139, Total Fat 5 g, Protein 8 g, Carbohydrate 16 g, Cholesterol 32 mg, Sodium 441 mg, Dietary Fiber <1 g Dietary Exchanges: 1 Bread, 1 Meat, ½ Fat

Mulled Wine

• •

2 bottles (750 ml each) dry
    red wine, such as
    Cabernet Sauvignon
1 cup light corn syrup
1 cup water
1 square (8 inches) double-
    thickness cheesecloth

Peel of 1 large orange
1 cinnamon stick, broken
    into halves
8 whole cloves
1 whole nutmeg
    Orange slices (optional)

COMBINE wine, corn syrup and water in slow cooker. Rinse
cheesecloth; squeeze out water. Wrap orange peel, cinnamon stick
halves, cloves and nutmeg in cheesecloth. Tie securely with cotton
string or strip of cheesecloth. Add to slow cooker. Cover and cook on
HIGH 2 to 2½ hours. Discard spice bag; ladle into glasses. Garnish
with orange slices, if desired.   *Makes 12 servings*

*Nutrients per Serving: Calories 179, Total Fat <1 g, Protein <1 g,
Carbohydrate 23 g, Cholesterol 0 mg, Sodium 31 mg, Dietary Fiber <1 g
Dietary Exchanges: 1½ Bread, 1½ Fat**

*Fat exchange accounts for the calories from the alcohol.

Main Courses

Southwest Turkey Tenderloin Stew

1 package (about
    1½ pounds) turkey
    tenderloins, cut into
    ¾-inch pieces
1 tablespoon chili powder
1 teaspoon ground cumin
¾ teaspoon salt
1 red bell pepper, cut into
    ¾-inch pieces
1 green bell pepper, cut into
    ¾-inch pieces
¾ cup chopped red or
    yellow onion

3 cloves garlic, minced
1 can (15½ ounces) chili
    beans in spicy sauce,
    undrained
1 can (14½ ounces) chili-
    style stewed tomatoes,
    undrained
¾ cup prepared salsa or
    picante sauce
    Fresh cilantro (optional)

PLACE turkey in slow cooker. Sprinkle chili powder, cumin and salt over turkey; toss to coat. Add red bell pepper, green bell pepper, onion, garlic, beans, tomatoes and salsa. Mix well. Cover and cook on LOW 5 hours or until turkey is no longer pink in centers and vegetables are crisp-tender. Ladle into bowls. Garnish with cilantro, if desired.

Makes 6 servings

Nutrients per Serving: Calories 228, Total Fat 4 g, Protein 25 g, Carbohydrate 27 g, Cholesterol 44 mg, Sodium 943 mg, Dietary Fiber 4 g
Dietary Exchanges: 2 Vegetable, 1 Bread, 2 Meat

Spareribs Simmered in Orange Sauce

4 pounds country-style
    pork spareribs
2 tablespoons vegetable oil
2 medium white onions, cut
    into ¼-inch slices
1 to 2 tablespoons dried
    ancho chilies, seeded
    and finely chopped
½ teaspoon ground
    cinnamon
¼ teaspoon ground cloves
1 can (16 ounces)
    tomatoes, undrained

2 cloves garlic
½ cup orange juice
⅓ cup dry white wine
⅓ cup packed brown sugar
1 teaspoon shredded
    orange peel
½ teaspoon salt
1 to 2 tablespoons cider
    vinegar
Orange wedges (optional)

TRIM excess fat from ribs. Cut into individual riblets. Heat oil in large skillet over medium heat. Add ribs; cook 10 minutes or until browned on all sides. Remove to plate. Remove and discard all but 2 tablespoons drippings from skillet. Add onions, chilies, cinnamon and ground cloves. Cook and stir 4 minutes or until softened. Transfer onion mixture to slow cooker.

PROCESS tomatoes with juices and garlic in food processor or blender until smooth.

COMBINE tomato mixture, orange juice, wine, sugar, orange peel and salt in slow cooker. Add ribs; stir to coat. Cover and cook on LOW 5 hours or until ribs are fork-tender. Remove ribs to plates. Ladle out liquid to medium bowl. Let stand 5 minutes. Skim and discard fat. Stir in vinegar; serve over ribs. Serve with carrots and garnish with orange wedges, if desired. *Makes 4 to 6 servings*

Nutrients per Serving: Calories 733, Total Fat 37 g, Protein 62 g, Carbohydrate 33 g, Cholesterol 125 mg, Sodium 575 mg, Dietary Fiber 3 g Dietary Exchanges: 2 Vegetable, ½ Fruit, 1 Bread, 9 Meat, 2 Fat

Bean Ragoût with Cilantro-Cornmeal Dumplings

2 cans (14½ ounces each) tomatoes, chopped and juice reserved
1½ cups chopped red bell pepper
1 large onion, chopped
1 can (15½ ounces) pinto or kidney beans, rinsed and drained
1 can (15½ ounces) black beans, rinsed and drained
2 small zucchini, sliced
½ cup chopped green bell pepper
½ cup chopped celery
1 poblano chili pepper,* seeded and chopped

2 cloves garlic, minced
3 tablespoons chili powder
2 teaspoons ground cumin
1 teaspoon dried oregano leaves
½ teaspoon salt, divided
⅛ teaspoon black pepper
¼ cup all-purpose flour
¼ cup yellow cornmeal
½ teaspoon baking powder
1 tablespoon vegetable shortening
2 tablespoons shredded Cheddar cheese
2 teaspoons minced fresh cilantro
¼ cup milk

COMBINE tomatoes with juice, red bell pepper, onion, beans, zucchini, green bell pepper, celery, poblano pepper, garlic, chili powder, cumin, oregano, ¼ teaspoon salt and black pepper in slow cooker; mix well. Cover and cook on LOW 7 to 8 hours.

PREPARE dumplings 1 hour before serving. Mix flour, cornmeal, baking powder and remaining ¼ teaspoon salt in medium bowl. Cut in shortening with pastry blender or two knives until mixture resembles coarse crumbs. Stir in cheese and cilantro. Pour milk into flour mixture. Blend just until dry ingredients are moistened. Turn slow cooker to HIGH. Drop dumplings by level tablespoonfuls (larger dumplings will not cook properly) on top of ragoût. Cover and cook 1 hour or until toothpick inserted in dumpling comes out clean.

Makes 6 servings

*Chili peppers can sting and irritate the skin; wear rubber gloves when handling peppers and do not touch eyes.

Nutrients per Serving: Calories 294, Total Fat 6 g, Protein 17 g, Carbohydrate 54 g, Cholesterol 3 mg, Sodium 998 mg, Dietary Fiber 10 g
Dietary Exchanges: 2 Vegetable, 3 Bread, ½ Fat

Texas-Style Barbecued Brisket

1 beef brisket (3 to
    4 pounds), cut into
    halves, if necessary, to
    fit slow cooker
3 tablespoons
    Worcestershire sauce
1 tablespoon chili powder
1 teaspoon celery salt
1 teaspoon black pepper
1 teaspoon liquid smoke
2 cloves garlic, minced
2 bay leaves
    Barbecue Sauce (recipe
    follows)

TRIM excess fat from meat and discard. Place meat in resealable plastic food storage bag. Combine Worcestershire sauce, chili powder, celery salt, pepper, liquid smoke, garlic and bay leaves in small bowl. Spread mixture on all sides of meat; seal bag. Refrigerate 24 hours.

PLACE meat and marinade in slow cooker. Cover and cook on LOW 7 hours. *Meanwhile,* prepare Barbecue Sauce.

REMOVE meat from slow cooker and pour juices into 2-cup measure; let stand 5 minutes. Skim fat from juices. Remove and discard bay leaves. Stir 1 cup of defatted juices into Barbecue Sauce. Discard remaining juices. Return meat and Barbecue Sauce to slow cooker. Cover and cook 1 hour or until meat is fork-tender. Remove meat to cutting board. Cut across grain into ¼-inch-thick slices. Serve 2 to 3 tablespoons Barbecue Sauce over each serving.
Makes 10 to 12 servings

Barbecue Sauce

2 tablespoons vegetable oil
1 medium onion, chopped
2 cloves garlic, minced
1 cup ketchup
½ cup molasses
¼ cup cider vinegar
2 teaspoons chili powder
½ teaspoon dry mustard

HEAT oil in medium saucepan over medium heat. Add onion and garlic; cook until onion is tender. Add remaining ingredients. Simmer 5 minutes.
Makes 2½ cups

Nutrients per Serving: Calories 275, Total Fat 11 g, Protein 24 g, Carbohydrate 20 g, Cholesterol 73 mg, Sodium 658 mg, Dietary Fiber 1 g Dietary Exchanges: 1½ Bread, 3½ Meat

Tuscan Pasta

....

1 pound boneless skinless chicken breasts, cut into 1-inch pieces

1 can (15½ ounces) red kidney beans, rinsed and drained

1 can (15 ounces) tomato sauce

2 cans (14½ ounces each) Italian-style stewed tomatoes

1 jar (4½ ounces) sliced mushrooms, drained

1 medium green bell pepper, chopped

½ cup onion, chopped

½ cup celery, chopped

4 cloves garlic, minced

1 cup water

1 teaspoon dried Italian seasoning

6 ounces thin spaghetti, broken into halves

PLACE all ingredients except spaghetti in slow cooker. Cover and cook on LOW 4 hours or until vegetables are tender.

TURN to HIGH. Stir in spaghetti; cover. Stir again after 10 minutes. Cover and cook 45 minutes or until pasta is tender. Garnish with basil and bell pepper strips, if desired.   *Makes 8 servings*

Nutrients per Serving: Calories 272, Total Fat 2 g, Protein 23 g, Carbohydrate 42 g, Cholesterol 34 mg, Sodium 666 mg, Dietary Fiber 6 g
Dietary Exchanges: 3 Vegetable, 1½ Bread, 1½ Meat

Pork Stew

2 tablespoons vegetable oil, divided

3 pounds fresh lean boneless pork butt, cut into 1½-inch cubes

2 medium white onions, thinly sliced

3 cloves garlic, minced

1 teaspoon salt

1 teaspoon ground cumin

¾ teaspoon dried oregano leaves

1 can (8 ounces) tomatillos, drained and chopped *or* 1 cup husked and chopped fresh tomatillos

1 can (4 ounces) chopped green chilies, drained

½ cup reduced-sodium chicken broth

1 large tomato, peeled and coarsely chopped

¼ cup fresh cilantro, chopped *or* ½ teaspoon ground coriander

2 teaspoons lime juice

4 cups hot cooked white rice

½ cup toasted slivered almonds (optional)

HEAT 1 tablespoon oil in large skillet over medium heat. Add pork; cook 10 minutes or until browned on all sides. Remove and set aside. Heat remaining 1 tablespoon oil in skillet. Add onions, garlic, salt, cumin and oregano; cook and stir 2 minutes or until soft.

COMBINE pork, onion mixture and remaining ingredients except rice and almonds in slow cooker; mix well. Cover and cook on LOW 5 hours or until pork is tender and barely pink in centers. Serve over rice and sprinkle with almonds, if desired.   *Makes 10 servings*

Nutrients per Serving: Calories 377, Total Fat 17 g, Protein 32 g, Carbohydrate 23 g, Cholesterol 76 mg, Sodium 357 mg, Dietary Fiber 1 g
Dietary Exchanges: 1½ Bread, 4½ Meat, ½ Fat

Lamb in Dill Sauce

2 large potatoes, peeled
and cut into 1-inch
cubes
½ cup chopped onion
1½ teaspoons salt
½ teaspoon black pepper
½ teaspoon dried dill weed
or 4 sprigs fresh dill
1 bay leaf
2 pounds lean lamb stew
meat, cut into 1-inch
cubes

1 cup plus 3 tablespoons
water, divided
2 tablespoons all-purpose
flour
1 teaspoon sugar
2 tablespoons lemon juice
Fresh dill (optional)

LAYER ingredients in slow cooker in the following order: potatoes, onion, salt, pepper, dill weed, bay leaf, lamb and 1 cup water. Cover and cook on LOW 6 to 8 hours.

REMOVE lamb and potatoes with slotted spoon; cover and keep warm. Remove and discard bay leaf. Turn heat to HIGH. Stir flour and remaining 3 tablespoons water in small bowl until smooth. Add half of cooking juices and sugar. Mix well and return to slow cooker. Cover and cook 15 minutes. Stir in lemon juice. Return lamb and potatoes to slow cooker. Cover and cook 10 minutes or until heated through. Garnish with fresh dill, if desired.   *Makes 6 servings*

Nutrients per Serving: Calories 299, Total Fat 11 g, Protein 33 g, Carbohydrate 15 g, Cholesterol 108 mg, Sodium 649 mg, Dietary Fiber 1 g Dietary Exchanges: 1 Bread, 4 Meat

KITCHEN HOW-TO

Here's an easy way to mince fresh herbs. Put the herbs in a measuring cup. Place the point of kitchen scissors in the cup and snip until finely chopped.

Garden Vegetable Tabbouleh Stew

1 large onion, chopped
2 medium carrots, cut
 lengthwise into halves,
 then cut into 1-inch
 pieces
1 cup green beans, cut into
 1-inch pieces
2 medium green onions,
 thinly sliced
1 small zucchini (4 ounces),
 sliced
1 can (15½ ounces) chick-
 peas (garbanzo beans),
 rinsed and drained

2 cans (14½ ounces each)
 diced tomatoes,
 undrained
¼ teaspoon salt
⅛ teaspoon black pepper
1 box (6 to 7 ounces)
 tabbouleh mix
1½ cups water
¼ cup olive oil
 Sour cream (optional)
 Fresh mint (optional)

LAYER ingredients in slow cooker in the following order: onion, carrots, green beans, green onions, zucchini, chick-peas, tomatoes with juice, salt and pepper. Sprinkle tabbouleh mix over vegetables. Pour water and olive oil evenly over top. Cover and cook on LOW 6 to 8 hours or until vegetables are crisp-tender. Serve in bowls and garnish with sour cream and fresh mint, if desired.

Makes 4 servings

Nutrients per Serving: Calories 448, Total Fat 16 g, Protein 13 g, Carbohydrate 66 g, Cholesterol 0 mg, Sodium 1427 mg, Dietary Fiber 10 g
Dietary Exchanges: 4 Vegetable, 3 Bread, 3 Fat

Thai Turkey & Noodles

1 package (about
 1½ pounds) turkey
 tenderloins, cut into
 ¾-inch pieces
1 red bell pepper, cut into
 short, thin strips
1¼ cups reduced-sodium
 chicken broth, divided
¼ cup reduced-sodium soy
 sauce
3 cloves garlic, minced
¾ teaspoon crushed red
 pepper flakes

¼ teaspoon salt
2 tablespoons cornstarch
3 green onions, cut into
 ½-inch pieces
⅓ cup creamy or chunky
 peanut butter (not
 natural-style)
12 ounces hot cooked
 vermicelli pasta
¾ cup peanuts or cashews,
 chopped
¾ cup cilantro, chopped

PLACE turkey, bell pepper, 1 cup broth, soy sauce, garlic, red pepper flakes and salt in slow cooker. Cover and cook on LOW 3 hours.

MIX cornstarch with remaining ¼ cup broth in small bowl until smooth. Turn slow cooker to HIGH. Stir in green onions, peanut butter and cornstarch mixture. Cover and cook 30 minutes or until sauce is thickened and turkey is no longer pink in centers. Stir well. Serve over vermicelli. Sprinkle with peanuts and cilantro.

Makes 6 servings

Nutrients per Serving: *Calories 387, Total Fat 19 g, Protein 31 g, Carbohydrate 25 g, Cholesterol 44 mg, Sodium 1044 mg, Dietary Fiber 3 g Dietary Exchanges: 1½ Bread, 3½ Meat, 2 Fat*

Cook's Nook

If you don't have vermicelli on hand, try substituting ramen noodles. Discard the flavor packet from ramen soup mix and drop the noodles into boiling water. Cook the noodles 2 to 3 minutes or until just tender. Drain and serve hot.

Favorite Beef Stew

· ·

3 carrots, cut lengthwise into halves, then cut into 1-inch pieces
3 ribs celery, cut into 1-inch pieces
2 large potatoes, peeled and cut into ½-inch pieces
1½ cups chopped onions
3 cloves garlic, chopped
1 bay leaf
1½ tablespoons Worcestershire sauce
¾ teaspoon dried thyme leaves

¾ teaspoon dried basil leaves
½ teaspoon black pepper
2 pounds lean beef stew meat, cut into 1-inch pieces
1 can (14½ ounces) diced tomatoes, undrained
1 can (14½ ounces) reduced-sodium beef broth
¼ cup all-purpose flour
½ cup cold water

LAYER ingredients in slow cooker in the following order: carrots, celery, potatoes, onions, garlic, bay leaf, Worcestershire sauce, thyme, basil, pepper, beef, tomatoes with juice and broth. Cover and cook on LOW 8 to 9 hours.

REMOVE beef and vegetables to large serving bowl; cover and keep warm. Remove and discard bay leaf. Turn slow cooker to HIGH; cover. Mix flour and water in small bowl until smooth. Add ½ cup cooking liquid; mix well. Stir flour mixture into slow cooker. Cover and cook 15 minutes or until thickened. Pour sauce over beef and vegetables. Serve immediately. *Makes 6 to 8 servings*

Nutrients per Serving: Calories 364, Total Fat 8 g, Protein 43 g, Carbohydrate 29 g, Cholesterol 95 mg, Sodium 279 mg, Dietary Fiber 3 g Dietary Exchanges: 2 Vegetable, 1 Bread, 4½ Meat

Pork Chops with Jalapeño-Pecan Cornbread Stuffing

6 boneless loin pork chops,
   1 inch thick
   (1½ pounds)
¾ cup chopped onion
¾ cup chopped celery
½ cup coarsely chopped
   pecans
½ medium jalapeño pepper,*
   seeded and chopped

1 teaspoon rubbed sage
½ teaspoon dried rosemary
   leaves
⅛ teaspoon black pepper
4 cups unseasoned
   cornbread stuffing mix
1¼ cups reduced-sodium
   chicken broth
1 egg, lightly beaten

TRIM excess fat from pork and discard. Spray large skillet with nonstick cooking spray; heat over medium heat. Add pork; cook 10 minutes or until browned on all sides. Remove; set aside. Add onion, celery, pecans, jalapeño pepper, sage, rosemary and black pepper to skillet. Cook 5 minutes or until tender; set aside.

COMBINE cornbread stuffing mix, vegetable mixture and broth in medium bowl. Stir in egg. Spoon stuffing mixture into slow cooker. Arrange pork on top. Cover and cook on LOW about 5 hours or until pork is tender and barely pink in centers. Serve with vegetable salad, if desired. *Makes 6 servings*

*Jalapeño peppers can sting and irritate the skin; wear rubber gloves when handling peppers and do not touch eyes.

Tip: If you prefer a more moist dressing, increase the chicken broth to 1½ cups.

Nutrients per Serving: Calories 272, Total Fat 14 g, Protein 17 g, Carbohydrate 19 g, Cholesterol 75 mg, Sodium 380 mg, Dietary Fiber 1 g Dietary Exchanges: 1 Vegetable, 1 Bread, 2 Meat, 1½ Fat

Coq au Vin

....

4 thick slices bacon
2 cups frozen pearl onions, thawed
1 cup sliced button mushrooms
1 clove garlic, minced
1 teaspoon dried thyme leaves
⅛ teaspoon black pepper
6 boneless skinless chicken breast halves (about 2 pounds)

½ cup dry red wine
¾ cup reduced-sodium chicken broth
¼ cup tomato paste
3 tablespoons all-purpose flour
Hot cooked egg noodles (optional)

COOK bacon in medium skillet over medium heat. Drain and crumble. Layer ingredients in slow cooker in the following order: onions, bacon, mushrooms, garlic, thyme, pepper, chicken, wine and broth. Cover and cook on LOW 6 to 8 hours.

REMOVE chicken and vegetables; cover and keep warm. Ladle ½ cup cooking liquid into small bowl; allow to cool slightly. Turn slow cooker to HIGH; cover. Mix reserved liquid, tomato paste and flour until smooth. Return mixture to slow cooker; cover and cook 15 minutes or until thickened. Serve over egg noodles, if desired.

Makes 6 servings

Nutrients per Serving: Calories 283, Total Fat 6 g, Protein 37 g, Carbohydrate 15 g, Cholesterol 96 mg, Sodium 295 mg, Dietary Fiber 1 g Dietary Exchanges: 3 Vegetable, 4 Meat

Cook's Nook

Coq au Vin is a classic French dish that is made with bone-in chicken, salt pork or bacon, brandy, red wine and herbs. The dish originated when farmers needed a way to cook old chickens that could no longer breed. A slow, moist cooking method was needed to tenderize the tough old birds.

Menu

Coq au Vin

Garlic Mashed Potatoes

Sautéed Zucchini
and Tomatoes

Chocolate Angel
Food Cake

Chili Turkey Loaf

2 pounds ground turkey
1 cup chopped onion
⅔ cup Italian-style
    seasoned dry bread
    crumbs
½ cup chopped green bell
    pepper
½ cup chili sauce
4 cloves garlic, minced

2 eggs, lightly beaten
2 tablespoons horseradish
    mustard
1 teaspoon salt
½ teaspoon Italian
    seasoning
¼ teaspoon black pepper
    Prepared salsa (optional)

MAKE foil handles for loaf using technique on page 10. Mix all ingredients except salsa in large bowl. Shape into round loaf and place on top of foil strips. Transfer to bottom of slow cooker using foil handles. Cover and cook on LOW 4½ to 5 hours or until temperature is 170°F. Remove loaf from slow cooker using foil handles. Place on serving plate. Let stand 5 minutes before serving. Cut into wedges and top with salsa, if desired. Serve with steamed carrots, if desired.

Makes 8 servings

Nutrients per Serving: Calories 263, Total Fat 13 g, Protein 23 g, Carbohydrate 12 g, Cholesterol 110 mg, Sodium 733 mg, Dietary Fiber 1 g
Dietary Exchanges: 1 Bread, 3 Meat, ½ Fat

Mediterranean Stew

1 medium butternut or acorn squash, peeled and cut into 1-inch cubes

2 cups unpeeled eggplant, cut into 1-inch cubes

2 cups sliced zucchini

1 can (15½ ounces) chick-peas (garbanzo beans), rinsed and drained

1 package (10 ounces) frozen cut okra

1 can (8 ounces) tomato sauce

1 cup chopped onion

1 medium tomato, chopped

1 medium carrot, thinly sliced

½ cup reduced-sodium vegetable broth

⅓ cup raisins

1 clove garlic, minced

½ teaspoon ground cumin

½ teaspoon ground turmeric

¼ to ½ teaspoon ground red pepper

¼ teaspoon ground cinnamon

¼ teaspoon paprika

6 to 8 cups hot cooked couscous or rice

Fresh parsley (optional)

COMBINE all ingredients except couscous and parsley in slow cooker; mix well. Cover and cook on LOW 8 to 10 hours or until vegetables are crisp-tender. Serve over couscous. Garnish with parsley, if desired.

Makes 6 servings

Nutrients per Serving: Calories 377, Total Fat 2 g, Protein 14 g, Carbohydrate 78 g, Cholesterol 0 mg, Sodium 508 mg, Dietary Fiber 16 g
Dietary Exchanges: 3 Vegetable, 4 Bread

Cook's Nook

Butternut squash is a member of the winter squash family. It is low in calories, fat and sodium. Although all squash are a good source of beta-carotene, winter squash develops additional beta-carotene after it has been picked and stored.

Veggie Mac and Tuna

· ·

1½ cups (6 ounces) elbow
    macaroni, uncooked
3 tablespoons butter or
    margarine
1 small onion, chopped
½ medium red bell pepper,
    chopped
½ medium green bell
    pepper, chopped
¼ cup all-purpose flour

1¾ cups milk
8 ounces cubed light
    pasteurized process
    cheese product
½ teaspoon dried marjoram
    leaves
1 package (10 ounces)
    frozen peas
1 can (9 ounces) tuna in
    water, drained

COOK macaroni according to package directions until just tender; drain. Melt butter in medium saucepan over medium heat. Add onion and bell peppers. Cook and stir 5 minutes or until tender. Add flour. Stir constantly over medium heat 2 minutes. Stir in milk and bring to a boil. Boil, stirring constantly, until thickened. Reduce heat to low; add cheese and marjoram. Stir until cheese is melted.

COMBINE macaroni, cheese sauce, peas and tuna in slow cooker. Cover and cook on LOW 2½ hours or until bubbly at edge.

Makes 6 servings

Nutrients per Serving: Calories 446, Total Fat 20 g, Protein 29 g, Carbohydrate 38 g, Cholesterol 69 mg, Sodium 821 mg, Dietary Fiber 3 g
Dietary Exchanges: 1 Vegetable, 2 Bread, 3 Meat, 2½ Fat

Yankee Pot Roast and Vegetables

1 beef chuck pot roast
  (2½ pounds)
3 medium baking potatoes
  (about 1 pound),
  unpeeled and cut into
  quarters
2 large carrots, cut into
  ¾-inch slices
2 ribs celery, cut into
  ¾-inch slices

1 medium onion, sliced
1 large parsnip, cut into
  ¾-inch slices
2 bay leaves
1 teaspoon dried rosemary
  leaves
½ teaspoon dried thyme
  leaves
½ cup reduced-sodium beef
  broth

TRIM excess fat from meat and discard. Cut into serving pieces;
sprinkle with salt and pepper. Combine vegetables, bay leaves,
rosemary and thyme in slow cooker. Place beef over vegetables in
slow cooker. Pour broth over beef. Cover and cook on LOW 8½ to
9 hours or until beef is fork-tender. Remove beef to serving platter.
Arrange vegetables around beef. Remove and discard bay leaves.

Makes 6 servings

Nutrients per Serving: Calories 494, Total Fat 17 g, Protein 48 g,
Carbohydrate 35 g, Cholesterol 124 mg, Sodium 139 mg, Dietary Fiber 2 g
Dietary Exchanges: 1 Vegetable, 2 Bread, 6 Meat

Cook's Nook

*To make gravy, ladle the juice into a
2-cup measure; let stand 5 minutes. Skim off and
discard the fat. Measure remaining juice and heat
to a boil in small saucepan. For each cup of juice,
mix 2 tablespoons of flour with ¼ cup of cold
water until smooth. Stir flour mixture into boiling
juice. Stir constantly 1 minute or until thickened.*

Menu
....

Yankee Pot Roast and Vegetables

Tossed Green Salad

Boston Brown Bread
(page 86)

Apple Pie

Lentil Stew over Couscous

1 large onion, chopped
1 green bell pepper, chopped
4 ribs celery, chopped
1 medium carrot, cut lengthwise into halves, then cut into 1-inch pieces
2 cloves garlic, chopped
3 cups lentils (1 pound), rinsed
1 can (14½ ounces) diced tomatoes, undrained
1 can (14½ ounces) reduced-sodium chicken broth
3 cups water
¼ teaspoon black pepper
1 teaspoon dried marjoram leaves
1 tablespoon cider vinegar
1 tablespoon olive oil
4½ to 5 cups hot cooked couscous
Carrot curls (optional)
Celery leaves (optional)

COMBINE onion, green bell pepper, celery, carrot, garlic, lentils, tomatoes with juice, broth, water, black pepper and marjoram in slow cooker. Stir; cover and cook on LOW 8 to 9 hours.

STIR in vinegar and olive oil. Serve over couscous. Garnish with carrot curls and celery leaves, if desired. *Makes 12 servings*

Tip: Lentil stew keeps well in the refrigerator for up to one week. Stew can also be frozen in airtight container in freezer for up to three months.

Nutrients per Serving: Calories 203, Total Fat 2 g, Protein 11 g, Carbohydrate 37 g, Cholesterol 0 mg, Sodium 128 mg, Dietary Fiber 4 g Dietary Exchanges: 1 Vegetable, 2 Bread, ½ Meat

Forty-Clove Chicken

1 frying chicken
(3 pounds), cut into
serving pieces
1 to 2 tablespoons olive oil
¼ cup dry white wine
⅛ cup dry vermouth
2 tablespoons chopped
fresh parsley *or*
2 teaspoons dried
parsley leaves
2 teaspoons dried basil
leaves

1 teaspoon dried oregano
leaves
Pinch of crushed red
pepper flakes
40 cloves garlic (about
2 heads), peeled
4 ribs celery, sliced
Juice and peel of 1 lemon
Fresh herbs (optional)

REMOVE skin from chicken, if desired. Sprinkle with salt and pepper.
Heat oil in large skillet over medium heat. Add chicken; cook
10 minutes or until browned on all sides. Remove to platter.

COMBINE wine, vermouth, parsley, basil, oregano and red pepper
flakes in large bowl. Add garlic and celery; coat well. Transfer garlic
and celery to slow cooker with slotted spoon. Add chicken to herb
mixture; coat well. Place chicken on top of vegetables in slow cooker.
Sprinkle lemon juice and peel in slow cooker; add remaining herb
mixture. Cover and cook on LOW 6 hours or until chicken is no
longer pink in centers. Garnish with fresh herbs, if desired.

Makes 4 to 6 servings

*Nutrients per Serving: Calories 416, Total Fat 20 g, Protein 41 g,
Carbohydrate 14 g, Cholesterol 139 mg, Sodium 173 mg, Dietary Fiber 1 g
Dietary Exchanges: 2 Vegetable, 6 Meat, ½ Fat*

Cook's Nook

*Peeling 40 cloves of garlic is easy if
you first separate the cloves from the head and
then drop them into boiling water for 30
seconds. Drain, wait until the garlic is cool to the
touch and slip the peels off with your fingers.*

Soups & Side Dishes

Green Beans with Savory Mushroom Sauce

2 packages (10 ounces each) frozen French-style green beans, thawed
1 can (10¾ ounces) condensed cream of mushroom soup, undiluted
¼ cup dry vermouth or dry white wine

4 ounces (1½ cups) fresh mushrooms, sliced
½ teaspoon salt
½ teaspoon dried thyme leaves
¼ teaspoon black pepper
1 cup crushed prepared croutons or canned fried onion rings

COMBINE all ingredients except croutons in slow cooker. Mix until well blended. Cover and cook on LOW 3 to 4 hours or until beans are crisp-tender. Sprinkle with croutons. Serve warm.

Makes 6 to 8 servings

Nutrients per Serving: Calories 159, Total Fat 5 g, Protein 5 g, Carbohydrate 22 g, Cholesterol 25 mg, Sodium 717 mg, Dietary Fiber < 1 g
Dietary Exchanges: 2 Vegetable, 1 Bread, 1 Fat

Russian Borscht

4 cups thinly sliced green
    cabbage
1½ pounds fresh beets,
    shredded
5 small carrots, peeled, cut
    lengthwise into halves,
    then cut into 1-inch
    pieces
1 parsnip, peeled, cut
    lengthwise into halves,
    then cut into 1-inch
    pieces
1 cup chopped onion
4 cloves garlic, minced

1 pound lean beef stew
    meat, cut into ½-inch
    cubes
1 can (14½ ounces) diced
    tomatoes, undrained
3 cans (14½ ounces each)
    reduced-sodium beef
    broth
¼ cup lemon juice
1 tablespoon sugar
1 teaspoon black pepper
    Sour cream (optional)
    Fresh parsley (optional)

LAYER ingredients in slow cooker in the following order: cabbage, beets, carrots, parsnip, onion, garlic, beef, tomatoes with juice, broth, lemon juice, sugar and pepper. Cover and cook on LOW 7 to 9 hours or until vegetables are crisp-tender. Season with additional lemon juice and sugar, if desired. Dollop with sour cream and garnish with parsley, if desired.

Makes 12 servings

Nutrients per Serving: Calories 128, Total Fat 2 g, Protein 13 g, Carbohydrate 15 g, Cholesterol 24 mg, Sodium 146 mg, Dietary Fiber 2 g
Dietary Exchanges: 3 Vegetable, 1½ Meat

Cook's Nook

Instead of slicing the cabbage with a knife, you can shred it with the large shredder holes of a four-sided grater or in a food processor.

Bean Pot Medley

1 can (15½ ounces) black beans, rinsed and drained

1 can (15½ ounces) red beans, rinsed and drained

1 can (15½ ounces) Great Northern beans, rinsed and drained

1 can (15½ ounces) black-eyed peas, rinsed and drained

1 can (8½ ounces) baby lima beans, rinsed and drained

1½ cups ketchup

1 cup chopped onion

1 cup chopped red bell pepper

1 cup chopped green bell pepper

½ cup packed brown sugar

½ cup water

2 to 3 teaspoons cider vinegar

1 teaspoon dry mustard

2 bay leaves

⅛ teaspoon black pepper

COMBINE all ingredients in slow cooker; stir. Cover and cook on LOW 6 to 7 hours or until onion and peppers are tender. Remove and discard bay leaves. *Makes 8 servings*

Nutrients per Serving: Calories 375, Total Fat 4 g, Protein 19 g, Carbohydrate 77 g, Cholesterol 0 mg, Sodium 1132 mg, Dietary Fiber 12 g
Dietary Exchanges: 5 Bread, ½ Fat

Mediterranean Gumbo

1 medium onion, chopped
½ medium green bell
    pepper, chopped
2 cloves garlic, minced
1 can (14½ ounces) whole
    tomatoes, undrained
    and coarsely chopped
2 cans (14½ ounces each)
    reduced-sodium
    chicken broth
1 can (8 ounces) tomato
    sauce
1 jar (2½ ounces) sliced
    mushrooms

¼ cup ripe olives, sliced
½ cup orange juice
½ cup dry white wine
    (optional)
2 bay leaves
1 teaspoon dried basil
    leaves
¼ teaspoon fennel seed,
    crushed
⅛ teaspoon black pepper
1 pound medium shrimp,
    peeled

PLACE all ingredients except shrimp in slow cooker. Cover and cook on LOW 4 to 4½ hours or until vegetables are crisp-tender. Stir in shrimp. Cover and cook 15 to 30 minutes or until shrimp are opaque. Remove and discard bay leaves.   *Makes 6 servings*

Nutrients per Serving: Calories 144, Total Fat 3 g, Protein 17 g, Carbohydrate 12 g, Cholesterol 117 mg, Sodium 869 mg, Dietary Fiber 2 g
Dietary Exchanges: 1½ Vegetable, 1½ Meat

Cook's Nook

If you prefer a hearty soup, add more seafood. Cut 1 pound of whitefish or cod into 1-inch pieces. Add the fish to your slow cooker 45 minutes before serving. Cover and cook on LOW.

Rustic Potatoes au Gratin

½ cup milk
1 can (10¾ ounces)
    condensed Cheddar
    cheese soup, undiluted
1 package (8 ounces)
    cream cheese, softened
1 clove garlic, minced

¼ teaspoon ground nutmeg
⅛ teaspoon black pepper
2 pounds baking potatoes,
    cut into ¼-inch slices
1 small onion, thinly sliced
    Paprika (optional)

HEAT milk in small saucepan over medium heat until small bubbles form around edge of pan. Remove from heat. Add soup, cheese, garlic, nutmeg and pepper. Stir until smooth. Layer ¼ of potatoes and onion on bottom of slow cooker. Top with ¼ of soup mixture. Repeat layers 3 times. Cover and cook on LOW 6½ to 7 hours or until potatoes are tender and most of liquid is absorbed. Sprinkle with paprika, if desired.   *Makes 6 servings*

Variation: Potatoes may be peeled, if desired.

Nutrients per Serving: Calories 421, Total Fat 17 g, Protein 10 g, Carbohydrate 59 g, Cholesterol 53 mg, Sodium 503 mg, Dietary Fiber <1 g Dietary Exchanges: 4 Bread, 3 Fat

Savory Pea Soup with Sausage

8 ounces smoked sausage,
cut lengthwise into
halves, then cut into
½-inch pieces
1 package (16 ounces)
dried split peas, rinsed
3 medium carrots, sliced
2 ribs celery, sliced

1 medium onion, chopped
¾ teaspoon dried marjoram
leaves
1 bay leaf
2 cans (14½ ounces each)
reduced-sodium
chicken broth

HEAT small skillet over medium heat. Add sausage; cook 5 to 8 minutes or until browned. Drain well. Combine sausage and remaining ingredients in slow cooker. Cover and cook on LOW 4 to 5 hours or until peas are tender. Turn off heat. Remove and discard bay leaf. Cover and let stand 15 minutes to thicken.

Makes 6 servings

Nutrients per Serving: Calories 424, Total Fat 13 g, Protein 27 g, Carbohydrate 53 g, Cholesterol 26 mg, Sodium 585 mg, Dietary Fiber 5 g
Dietary Exchanges: 1 Vegetable, 3 Bread, 2 Meat, 1½ Fat

Cook's Nook

Wondering what type of sausage to use? Try kielbasa or chorizo. If you prefer, smoked ham would be a good sausage substitute.

Chicken and Vegetable Chowder

1 pound boneless skinless
   chicken breasts, cut
   into 1-inch pieces
10 ounces frozen broccoli
   cuts
1 cup sliced carrots
½ cup chopped onion
½ cup whole kernel corn
1 jar (4½ ounces) sliced
   mushrooms, drained

2 cloves garlic, minced
½ teaspoon dried thyme
   leaves
1 can (14½ ounces)
   reduced-sodium
   chicken broth
1 can (10¾ ounces)
   condensed cream of
   potato soup
⅓ cup half-and-half

COMBINE all ingredients except half-and-half in slow cooker. Cover and cook on LOW 5 hours or until vegetables are tender and chicken is no longer pink in centers. Stir in half-and-half. Turn to HIGH. Cover and cook 15 minutes or until heated through.   *Makes 6 servings*

Variation: If desired, ½ cup (2 ounces) shredded Swiss or Cheddar cheese can be added. Add to thickened broth, stirring over LOW heat until melted.

Nutrients per Serving: Calories 188, Total Fat 5 g, Protein 22 g, Carbohydrate 15 g, Cholesterol 54 mg, Sodium 704 mg, Dietary Fiber 2 g Dietary Exchanges: 1 Bread, 2 Meat

Risi Bisi

....

1½ cups converted long
    grain white rice
¾ cup chopped onion
2 cloves garlic, minced
2 cans (14½ ounces each)
    reduced-sodium
    chicken broth
⅓ cup water
¾ teaspoon Italian
    seasoning

½ teaspoon dried basil
    leaves
½ cup frozen peas, thawed
¼ cup grated Parmesan
    cheese
¼ cup toasted pine nuts
    (optional)

COMBINE rice, onion and garlic in slow cooker. Heat broth and water in small saucepan to a boil. Stir boiling liquid, Italian seasoning and basil into rice mixture. Cover and cook on LOW 2 to 3 hours or until liquid is absorbed. Add peas. Cover and cook 1 hour. Stir in cheese. Spoon rice into serving bowl. Sprinkle with pine nuts, if desired.

Makes 6 servings

Nutrients per Serving: *Calories 222, Total Fat 2 g, Protein 9 g, Carbohydrate 42 g, Cholesterol 3 mg, Sodium 295 mg, Dietary Fiber 1 g Dietary Exchanges: 3 Bread*

Cook's Nook

Risi Bisi ("rice and peas") is a traditional Italian dish. It is said to be the first dish served each April 29th at the Venetian feasts honoring St. Mark. Small Italian peas are sweetest and most tender at that time of year.

Minestrone alla Milanese

2 cans (14½ ounces each) reduced-sodium beef broth
1 can (14½ ounces) diced tomatoes, undrained
1 cup diced potato
1 cup coarsely chopped green cabbage
1 cup coarsely chopped carrots
1 cup sliced zucchini
¾ cup chopped onion
¾ cup sliced fresh green beans
¾ cup coarsely chopped celery

¾ cup water
2 tablespoons olive oil
1 clove garlic, minced
½ teaspoon dried basil leaves
¼ teaspoon dried rosemary leaves
1 bay leaf
1 can (15½ ounces) cannellini beans, rinsed and drained
Grated Parmesan cheese (optional)

COMBINE all ingredients except cannellini beans and cheese in slow cooker; mix well. Cover and cook on LOW 5 to 6 hours. Add cannellini beans. Cover and cook on LOW 1 hour or until vegetables are crisp-tender. Remove and discard bay leaf. Garnish with cheese, if desired. *Makes 8 to 10 servings*

Nutrients per Serving: Calories 135, Total Fat 4 g, Protein 8 g, Carbohydrate 23 g, Cholesterol 0 mg, Sodium 242 mg, Dietary Fiber 5 g Dietary Exchanges: 1½ Vegetable, 1 Bread, ½ Fat

Orange-Spice Glazed Carrots

1 package (32 ounces)
  baby carrots
½ cup packed brown sugar
½ cup orange juice
3 tablespoons butter or
  margarine

¾ teaspoon ground
  cinnamon
¼ teaspoon ground nutmeg
2 tablespoons cornstarch
¼ cup water

COMBINE all ingredients except cornstarch and water in slow cooker. Cover and cook on LOW 3½ to 4 hours or until carrots are crisp-tender. Spoon carrots into serving bowl. Remove juices to small saucepan. Heat to a boil. Mix cornstarch and water in small bowl until blended. Stir into saucepan. Boil 1 minute or until thickened, stirring constantly. Pour over carrots.   *Makes 6 servings*

Nutrients per Serving: Calories 193, Total Fat 6 g, Protein 2 g, Carbohydrate 35 g, Cholesterol 15 mg, Sodium 153 mg, Dietary Fiber <1 g Dietary Exchanges: 2 Vegetable, 1½ Bread, 1 Fat

Navy Bean Bacon Chowder

1½ cups dried navy beans,
    rinsed
2 cups cold water
6 thick slices bacon
1 medium carrot, cut
    lengthwise into halves,
    then cut into 1-inch
    pieces
1 rib celery, chopped
1 medium onion, chopped

1 small turnip, cut into
    1-inch pieces
1 teaspoon dried Italian
    seasoning
⅛ teaspoon black pepper
1 large can (46 ounces)
    reduced-sodium
    chicken broth
1 cup milk

SOAK beans overnight in cold water.

COOK bacon in medium skillet over medium heat. Drain and crumble. Combine carrot, celery, onion, turnip, Italian seasoning, pepper, beans and bacon in slow cooker; mix slightly. Pour broth over top. Cover and cook on LOW 7½ to 9 hours or until beans are crisp-tender.

LADLE 2 cups of soup mixture into food processor or blender. Process until smooth; return to slow cooker. Add milk; cover and heat on HIGH 10 minutes or until heated through.   *Makes 6 servings*

Nutrients per Serving: Calories 270, Total Fat 5 g, Protein 20 g, Carbohydrate 39 g, Cholesterol 8 mg, Sodium 470 mg, Dietary Fiber 1 g
Dietary Exchanges: 1 Vegetable, 2 Bread, 1 Meat, 1 Fat

Breads & Desserts

Steamed Southern Sweet Potato Custard

1 can (16 ounces) cut sweet
   potatoes, drained
1 can (12 ounces)
   evaporated milk,
   divided
½ cup packed brown sugar
2 eggs, lightly beaten

1 teaspoon ground
   cinnamon
½ teaspoon ground ginger
¼ teaspoon salt
   Whipped cream (optional)
   Ground nutmeg (optional)

PROCESS sweet potatoes with about ¼ cup milk in food processor or blender until smooth. Add remaining milk, brown sugar, eggs, cinnamon, ginger and salt; process until well mixed. Pour into ungreased 1-quart soufflé dish. Cover tightly with foil. Crumple large sheet (about 15×12 inches) of foil; place on bottom of slow cooker. Pour 2 cups water over foil. Make foil handles using technique on page 10. Place soufflé dish on top of foil strips.

TRANSFER dish to slow cooker using foil handles; lay foil strips over top of dish. Cover and cook on HIGH 2½ to 3 hours or until skewer inserted in center comes out clean. Using foil strips, lift dish from slow cooker and transfer to wire rack. Uncover; let stand 30 minutes. Garnish with whipped cream and nutmeg, if desired.

Makes 4 servings

Nutrients per Serving: Calories 372, Total Fat 9 g, Protein 11 g, Carbohydrate 62 g, Cholesterol 131 mg, Sodium 351 mg, Dietary Fiber 2 g
Dietary Exchanges: ½ Milk, 3½ Bread, 2 Fat

Fruit & Nut Baked Apples

4 large baking apples, such
   as Rome Beauty or
   Cortland
1 tablespoon lemon juice
⅓ cup chopped dried
   apricots
⅓ cup chopped walnuts or
   pecans

3 tablespoons packed
   brown sugar
½ teaspoon ground
   cinnamon
2 tablespoons melted
   butter or margarine

SCOOP out center of each apple, leaving 1½-inch-wide cavity about ½ inch from bottom. Peel top of apple down about 1 inch. Brush peeled edges evenly with lemon juice. Mix apricots, walnuts, brown sugar and cinnamon in small bowl. Add butter; mix well. Spoon mixture evenly into apple cavities.

POUR ½ cup water onto bottom of slow cooker. Place 2 apples in slow cooker. Arrange remaining 2 apples above but not directly on top of bottom apples. Cover and cook on LOW 3 to 4 hours or until apples are tender. Serve warm or at room temperature with caramel ice cream topping, if desired. *Makes 4 servings*

Nutrients per Serving: Calories 260, Total Fat 12 g, Protein 3 g, Carbohydrate 40 g, Cholesterol 15 mg, Sodium 64 mg, Dietary Fiber 4 g Dietary Exchanges: 2½ Fruit, 2½ Fat

Cook's Nook

Ever wonder why you need to brush lemon juice onto apples to keep them from browning? Citrus fruits contain an acid that keeps apples, potatoes and other white vegetables from discoloring once they are cut or peeled.

Boston Brown Bread

3 (16-ounce) emptied and
    cleaned cans
½ cup rye flour
½ cup yellow cornmeal
½ cup whole wheat flour
3 tablespoons sugar

1 teaspoon baking soda
¾ teaspoon salt
½ cup chopped walnuts
½ cup raisins
1 cup buttermilk*
⅓ cup molasses

SPRAY cans and 1 side of three 6-inch-square pieces of aluminum foil with nonstick cooking spray; set aside. Combine rye flour, cornmeal, whole wheat flour, sugar, baking soda and salt in large bowl. Stir in walnuts and raisins. Whisk buttermilk and molasses in medium bowl until blended. Add buttermilk mixture to dry ingredients; stir until well mixed. Spoon mixture evenly into prepared cans. Place 1 piece of foil, greased side down, on top of each can. Secure foil with rubber bands or cotton string.

PLACE filled cans in slow cooker. Pour enough boiling water into slow cooker to come halfway up sides of cans. (Make sure foil tops do not touch boiling water.) Cover and cook on LOW 4 hours or until skewer inserted in centers comes out clean. To remove bread, lay cans on side; roll and tap gently on all sides until bread releases. Cool completely on wire racks.   *Makes 3 loaves*

*Soured fresh milk may be substituted. To sour, place 1 tablespoon lemon juice plus enough milk to equal 1 cup in 2-cup measure. Stir; let stand 5 minutes before using.

Nutrients per Serving: Calories 93, Total Fat 2 g, Protein 2 g, Carbohydrate 17 g, Cholesterol <1 mg, Sodium 181 mg, Dietary Fiber 2 g Dietary Exchanges: 1 Bread, ½ Fat

Poached Pears with Raspberry Sauce

4 cups cran-raspberry juice
    cocktail
2 cups Rhine or Riesling
    wine
¼ cup sugar
2 cinnamon sticks, broken
    into halves

4 to 5 firm Bosc or Anjou
    pears, peeled, cored
    and seeded
1 package (10 ounces)
    frozen raspberries in
    syrup, thawed
Fresh berries (optional)

COMBINE juice, wine, sugar and cinnamon stick halves in slow cooker. Submerge pears in mixture. Cover and cook on LOW 3½ to 4 hours or until pears are tender. Remove and discard cinnamon sticks.

PROCESS raspberries in food processor or blender until smooth; strain out seeds. Spoon raspberry sauce onto serving plates; place pear on top of sauce. Garnish with fresh berries, if desired.

Makes 4 to 5 servings

Nutrients per Serving: Calories 429, Total Fat 1 g, Protein 1 g, Carbohydrate 90 g, Cholesterol 0 mg, Sodium 18 mg, Dietary Fiber 7 g Dietary Exchanges: 6 Fruit, 1½ Fat*

*Fat exchange accounts for the calories from the alcohol.

Cook's Nook

Vary the look of this dessert by leaving some peel on the pears. To make stripes, peel off a curved strip using a vegetable peeler or paring knife, then leave the next strip of peel on the pear. Continue until you've gone all the way around the pear. After poaching, the remaining strips of peel can be removed from the pear to reveal the white flesh. The sections that were peeled before poaching will be pink.

English Bread Pudding

16 slices day-old, firm-
 textured white bread
 (1 small loaf)
1¾ cups milk
 1 package (8 ounces)
 mixed dried fruit, cut
 into small pieces
 ½ cup chopped nuts
 1 medium apple, cored and
 chopped

¼ cup butter or margarine,
 melted
⅓ cup packed brown sugar
 1 egg, lightly beaten
 1 teaspoon ground
 cinnamon
 ¼ teaspoon ground nutmeg
 ¼ teaspoon ground cloves

TEAR bread, with crusts, into 1- to 2-inch pieces. Place in slow cooker. Pour milk over bread; let soak 30 minutes. Stir in dried fruit, nuts and apple. Combine remaining ingredients in small bowl. Pour over bread mixture. Stir well to blend. Cover and cook on LOW 3½ to 4 hours or until skewer inserted in center comes out clean.

Makes 6 to 8 servings

Nutrients per Serving: *Calories 516, Total Fat 19 g, Protein 12 g, Carbohydrate 80 g, Cholesterol 61 mg, Sodium 446 mg, Dietary Fiber 5 g*
Dietary Exchanges: 3 Fruit, 2 Bread, 1 Meat, 3 Fat

Cook's Nook

Chopping dried fruits can be difficult. To make the job easier, cut the fruit with kitchen scissors. You can also spray your scissors or chef's knife with nonstick cooking spray before you begin chopping so that the fruit won't stick to the blade.

Spiced Apple & Cranberry Compote

1 package (6 ounces) dried
   apples
½ cup (2 ounces) dried
   cranberries
2½ cups cranberry juice
   cocktail
½ cup Rhine wine or apple
   juice

½ cup honey
2 cinnamon sticks, broken
   into halves
Frozen yogurt or ice
   cream (optional)
Additional cinnamon
   sticks (optional)

MIX apples, cranberries, juice, wine, honey and cinnamon stick halves in slow cooker. Cover and cook on LOW 4 to 5 hours or until liquid is absorbed and fruit is tender. Remove and discard cinnamon stick halves. Ladle compote into bowls. Serve warm, at room temperature or chilled with scoop of frozen yogurt. Garnish with additional cinnamon sticks, if desired. *Makes 6 servings*

Nutrients per Serving: Calories 238, Total Fat <1 g, Protein <1 g, Carbohydrate 59 g, Cholesterol 0 mg, Sodium 31 mg, Dietary Fiber 4 g
Dietary Exchanges: 4 Fruit

Barbecued Meatballs, 20
Bean Pot Medley, 64
Bean Ragoût with Cilantro-Cornmeal
    Dumplings, 28
Beef
    Barbecued Meatballs, 20
    Favorite Beef Stew, 42
    Texas-Style Barbecued Brisket,
      30
    Yankee Pot Roast and Vegetables,
      54

Caponata, 12
Chicken
    Chicken and Vegetable Chowder,
      72
    Coq au Vin, 46
    Forty-Clove Chicken, 58
    Tuscan Pasta, 32
Chili con Queso, 16
Chili Turkey Loaf, 48
Coq au Vin, 46

English Bread Pudding, 90

Favorite Beef Stew, 42
Fish and Shellfish
    Mediterranean Gumbo, 66
    Veggie Mac and Tuna, 52
Forty-Clove Chicken, 58
Fruit & Nut Baked Apples, 84

Garden Vegetable Tabbouleh Stew,
    38
Green Beans with Savory Mushroom
    Sauce, 60

Lamb in Dill Sauce, 36
Lentil Stew over Couscous, 56

Mediterranean Gumbo, 66
Mediterranean Stew, 50
Minestrone alla Milanese, 76
Mocha Supreme, 18
Mulled Apple Cider, 14
Mulled Wine, 22

Navy Bean Bacon Chowder, 80

Orange-Spice Glazed Carrots, 78

Pasta
    Coq au Vin, 46
    Lentil Stew over Couscous, 56
    Thai Turkey & Noodles, 40
    Tuscan Pasta, 32
    Veggie Mac and Tuna, 52
Poached Pears with Raspberry Sauce,
    88

Pork
    Pork Chops with Jalapeño-Pecan
      Cornbread Stuffing, 44
    Pork Stew, 34
    Spareribs Simmered in Orange Sauce, 26

Risi Bisi, 74
Russian Borscht, 62
Rustic Potatoes au Gratin, 68

Sauce, Barbecue, 30
Savory Pea Soup with Sausage, 70
Soups and Stews
    Bean Ragoût with Cilantro-Cornmeal
      Dumplings, 28
    Chicken and Vegetable Chowder, 72
    Chili con Queso, 16
    Coq au Vin, 46
    Favorite Beef Stew, 42
    Garden Vegetable Tabbouleh Stew, 38
    Lentil Stew over Couscous, 56
    Mediterranean Gumbo, 66
    Minestrone alla Milanese, 76
    Navy Bean Bacon Chowder, 80
    Pork Stew, 34
    Russian Borscht, 62
    Savory Pea Soup with Sausage, 70
    Southwest Turkey Tenderloin Stew, 24
Southwest Turkey Tenderloin Stew, 24
Spareribs Simmered in Orange Sauce, 26
Spiced Apple & Cranberry Compote, 92
Steamed Southern Sweet Potato Custard,
    82

Texas-Style Barbecued Brisket, 30
Thai Turkey & Noodles, 40
Turkey
    Chili Turkey Loaf, 48
    Southwest Turkey Tenderloin Stew, 24
    Thai Turkey & Noodles, 40
Tuscan Pasta, 32

Vegetables
    Bean Pot Medley, 64
    Bean Ragoût with Cilantro-Cornmeal
      Dumplings, 28
    Caponata, 12
    Green Beans with Savory Mushroom
      Sauce, 60
    Lentil Stew over Couscous, 56
    Mediterranean Stew, 50
    Minestrone alla Milanese, 76
    Navy Bean Bacon Chowder, 80
    Orange-Spice Glazed Carrots, 78
    Rustic Potatoes au Gratin, 68
    Savory Pea Soup with Sausage, 70
Veggie Mac and Tuna, 52

Yankee Pot Roast and Vegetables, 54